WORLD'S STRANGEST

PREDATORS

Produced for Lonely Planet by Plum5 Limited
Authors: Stuart Derrick & Charlotte Goddard
Editor: Plum5 Limited
Designer: Plum5 Limited
Publishing Director: Piers Pickard
Art Director: Andy Mansfield
Commissioning Editors: Catharine Robertson, Jen Feroze
Assistant Editor: Christina Webb
Print Production: Nigel Longuet, Lisa Ford
With thanks to: Jennifer Dixon

Published in August 2018 by Lonely Planet Global Ltd

CRN: 554153
ISBN: 978 1 78701 304 9

www.lonelyplanetkids.com
© Lonely Planet 2018

Printed in China
2 4 6 8 10 9 7 5 3 1

STAY IN TOUCH – lonelyplanet.com/contact
Lonely Planet Offices
AUSTRALIA the Malt Store, Level 3, 551 Swanston St, Carlton,
Victoria 3053   T: 03 8379 8000
IRELAND Digital Depot, Roe Lane (off Thomas St),
Digital Hub, Dublin 8, D08 TCV4
USA 124 Linden St, Oakland, CA 94607 T: 510 250 6400
UK 240 Blackfriars Rd, London SE1 8NW T: 020 3771 5100

WORLD'S STRANGEST

PREDATORS

Stuart Derrick &
Charlotte Goddard

PICTURE CREDITS

The Publisher would like to thank the following for their kind permission to reproduce their photographs:

Page 4–5: Shutterstock / Susan E. Viera; Page 6–7: Shutterstock / GoneWithTheWind; Page 8–9: Grant Heilman Photography / Alamy Stock Photo; Page 10–11: Getty images / Science Photo Library – PASIEKA; Page 11 inset: Shutterstock / Barbara Brockhauser; Page 12: Shutterstock / Thomas Wong; Page 12 inset: Shutterstock / Ian Redding; Page 13: Shutterstock / worldswildlifewonders; Page 14–15: Shutterstock / Jaime Pharr; Page 15 inset: Shutterstock / wael alreweie; Page 16: Shutterstock / Jinny Jin; Page 17: Getty images / Doxieone Photography; Page 18–19: Shutterstock / outdoorsman; Page 18 inset: Shutterstock / Ondrej Prosicky; Page 20: Getty images / Thomas P. Peschak; Page 21: Getty images / Giuseppe Sedda / REDA&CO / UIG; Page 22–23: Shutterstock / cineuno; Page 22 inset: Getty images / Doxieone Photography; Page 23 inset: Grant Heilman Photography / Alamy Stock Photo; Page 24–25: Shutterstock / Alfredo Maiquez; Page 25 inset: Shutterstock / Valdecasas; Page 26–27: Getty images / Matthijs Kuijpers; Page 27 inset: Shutterstock / Matt Jeppson; Page 28–29: Getty images / André De Kesel; Page 30: Shutterstock / belizar; Page 31: Getty images / Colin Zylka / EyeEm; Page 32–33: Shutterstock / kaschibo; Page 34: Terry Whittaker / Alamy Stock Photo; Page 35: ephotocorp / Alamy Stock Photo; Page 36–37: Shutterstock / Ariel Bravy; Page 38–39: Shutterstock / Milan Zygmunt; Page 40–41: Shutterstock / cineuno; Page 40 inset: Shutterstock / Alfredo Maiquez; Page 41 inset: Terry Whittaker / Alamy Stock Photo; Page 42–43: Getty images / Ali Trisno Pranoto; Page 44–45: Shutterstock / Ryan M. Bolton; Page 46: Getty images / CraigRJD; Page 47: Shutterstock / Vince Adam; Page 48–49: Getty images / Rebecca R Jackrel; Page 49 inset: Shutterstock / Galina Savina; Page 50–51: Getty images / Franco Banfi; Page 52: Getty images / Image Source; Page 53: Shutterstock / Ryan M. Bolton; Page 54–55: AfriPics.com / Alamy Stock Photo; Page 54 inset: Shutterstock / torikell; Page 56–57: Getty images / Birgitte Wilms/ Minden Pictures; Page 57 inset: Shutterstock / Mike Workman; Page 58–59: Shutterstock / cineuno; Page 58 inset: Shutterstock / Ryan M. Bolton; Page 59 inset: AfriPics.com / Alamy Stock Photo; Page 60–61: Shutterstock / Vladimir Wrangel; Page 62–63: Getty images / Anup Shah; Page 62 inset: WILDLIFE GmbH / Alamy Stock Photo; Page 64–65: Getty images / Vi Vien Lee; Page 65 inset: srijanrc travel / Alamy Stock Photo; Page 66: Getty images / Mark Newman; Page 67: BIOSPHOTO / Alamy Stock Photo; Page 68–69: Shutterstock / Piotr Krzeslak; Page 69 inset: Shutterstock / Wildlife World; Page 70–71: Minden Pictures / Alamy Stock Photo; Page 72–73: Shutterstock / aquapix; Page 74–75: Getty images / Eric Lowenbach; Page 74 inset: Getty images / Mark Moffett / Minden Pictures; Page 76–77: Shutterstock / Braam Collins; Page 76 inset: Getty images / Vincent Grafhorst / Minden Pictures; Page 78–79: Shutterstock / cineuno; Page 78 inset: Getty images / Anup Shah; Page 79 inset: Getty images / Eric Lowenbach; Page 80: Shutterstock / Susan E. Viera.

CONTENTS

INTRODUCTION

Every creature needs to eat to survive, and for some, that means eating other animals. To do this, they must be able to catch animals that really don't want to end up as dinner.

In this book, we've ranked the world's strangest predators to find out about...

⭐ The cunning ways they try to catch their prey

⭐ Their ferocity

⭐ Their beastly behavior

Read on to find out about the most bizarre and scary predators on the planet, including:

⭐ The plants that gobble up insects for lunch

⭐ The ferocious fish with a taste for flesh

⭐ Some of the most poisonous animals in the world

⭐ A real-life dragon that can tackle a buffalo

⭐ The snake with a unique disguise for luring birds into its clutches

... and many more!

STRANGEOMETER

The creatures in this book are all unique in their own ways, so we've used a special strangeometer to rank them. This is made up of four categories with a score out of 25 for each.

These categories are...

STRANGEOMETER

STRANGENESS		17/25
DANGER		8/25
CUNNING		12/25
FEROCITY		13/25
⭐ STRANGEOMETER SCORE		50/100

STRANGENESS

This examines how unusual the creature and its attack method are.

DANGER

How menacing is this creature to animals and humans?

CUNNING

If the creature uses sneaky skills to get its dinner, it will score well in this category.

FEROCITY

Some animals are simply very fierce. They will get big scores here.

STRANGEOMETER SCORE

These are added up to get a strangeometer score out of 100!

Short-tailed shrews must feed every two or three hours, eating several times their own weight each day.

MY TAIL IS ONLY ABOUT A QUARTER OF THE LENGTH OF MY BODY.

STRANGEOMETER

 STRANGENESS | 10/25

 DANGER | 10/25

CUNNING | 10/25

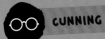 FEROCITY | 10/25

 STRANGEOMETER SCORE | 40/100

SHORT-TAILED SHREW

This tiny terror may be small and have weak jaws, but it is one of only a small number of mammals with venom glands. The venom, injected through its teeth, can stun or kill frogs and mice.

North America

The shrew has poor hearing and eyesight, so it detects its prey like a bat by using the echoes from high-pitched squeaks.

VENUS FLYTRAP

A plant that eats living things sounds scary, and it is – if you're a fly! Insects are attracted to the Venus flytrap by the scent of its sweet nectar, which is one of their favorite foods.

WHY DON'T YOU DROP IN FOR DINNER?

When a fly lands on the plant, it steps on tiny hairs, which lets the plant know that dinner has arrived. The plant then snaps its leaves shut, trapping the fly, before using its digestive juices to turn the fly into a soup.

STRANGEOMETER

 STRANGENESS — 20/25

 DANGER — 9/25

 CUNNING — 10/25

 FEROCITY — 2/25

 **STRANGEOMETER SCORE** — 41/100

The Venus flytrap doesn't just catch flies. It also eats ants, spiders, beetles, and grasshoppers. It takes the plant about ten days to digest its food.

East Coast of the US

Scientists have created robotic versions of Venus flytraps that can trap live insects.

I ALWAYS LEAVE A LIGHT ON.

Glowworms are actually not worms at all. The name is given to all kinds of glowing insects, including the larvae of flies and beetles, as well as beetles themselves.

Europe, Russia, India, Asia, New Zealand

The glowworm produces its light through a chemical reaction called bioluminescence. The glow acts as a warning to predators to stay away (glowworms taste horrible).

GLOWWORM

Glowworms weave a sticky web in the caves where they live, and their rear ends produce a strange blue light that attracts other insects. The insects become trapped in the web's sticky threads, and the glowworms can reel them in and eat them.

STRANGEOMETER

STRANGENESS		18/25
DANGER		6/25
CUNNING		15/25
FEROCITY		3/25
STRANGEOMETER SCORE		42/100

The platypus needs to be in the water for about 12 hours a day to catch enough food. It can store food in its cheeks while underwater. Once it surfaces, it chews with grinding pads, as it has no teeth. Despite its weird cuddliness, the platypus is venomous. Spurs on its hind feet can inject venom into predators and other platypuses.

#37

Australia

I LAY EGGS, EVEN THOUGH I'M A MAMMAL. WEIRD, HUH?

STRANGEOMETER

STRANGENESS	20/25
DANGER	10/25
CUNNING	7/25
FEROCITY	10/25
STRANGEOMETER SCORE	47/100

PLATYPUS

With its duck-like bill, webbed feet, and large tail, the platypus looks strange, and it has some unusual features for hunting. Its bill senses the movement of worms, fish, and shrimp in the water. The platypus is one of the few species of venomous mammals.

#36

COBRA LILY

The cobra lily (also called a pitcher plant) is a carnivorous plant that traps and digests insects. It can live in very hostile environments and can even survive fire.

Northern California and Oregon, US

STRANGEOMETER

 STRANGENESS — 19/25

 DANGER — 10/25

 CUNNING — 17/25

 FEROCITY — 2/25

 STRANGEOMETER SCORE — 48/100

Insects fly into the hooded top of the plant and become lost. Light at the back of the plant tricks the insects into thinking they have found the way out, but they end up falling into a funnel, where they become trapped and are eaten.

INSECTS GET EXHAUSTED TRYING TO FIND A WAY OUT, AND THEN THEY'RE ALL MINE!

The cobra lily gets its name because the shape of its hood resembles a rearing cobra. The dangling flowers even look like a snake's fangs or forked tongue.

PIRANHA

For its size, the piranha has one of the strongest bites of any animal, and its razor-sharp teeth are like those of a shark. It uses them to tear chunks of flesh from other fish or animals.

STRANGEOMETER

STRANGENESS		15/25
DANGER		13/25
CUNNING		8/25
FEROCITY		13/25
STRANGEOMETER SCORE		49/100

Piranhas scare off other fish by making a barking noise and using the muscles of their swim bladder to create an ominous drumming sound.

SOME PIRANHAS ARE ACTUALLY VEGETARIAN... BUT NOT ME!

shoal
piranhas
n feed on a large
mal, but usually only if the animal is
ng or already dead. Scientists think that piranhas are most
ly to attack in the dry season, when food is scarce and
er water levels bring more fish together.

South America

STRANGEOMETER

STRANGENESS	15/25	
DANGER	10/25	
CUNNING	16/25	
FEROCITY	10/25	
STRANGEOMETER SCORE	51/100	

When a green heron catches a large frog, it will drown it before swallowing it.

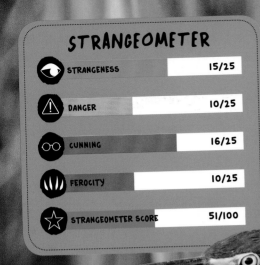

North America

I AM ONE OF THE FEW BIRDS THAT USES TOOLS.

GREEN HERON

Fishermen know that patience is required, and the green heron has lots when it comes to catching fish. It stands still in shallow water, waiting for fish to swim past, and then stretching out its neck to grab them.

The green heron has a clever trick to catch fish. First, it drops bait on top of the water. This can be twigs, insects, or even bread. When a fish comes to investigate, the heron pounces and snatches it with its razor-sharp bill.

#33

Arctic region

The white coat of the Arctic fox provides great winter camouflage, allowing it to blend into the snow and ice. When the seasons change, its coat becomes brown or gray to blend in with rocks and plants.

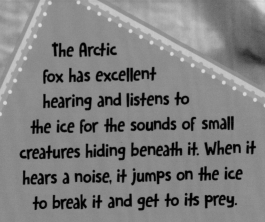

The Arctic fox has excellent hearing and listens to the ice for the sounds of small creatures hiding beneath it. When it hears a noise, it jumps on the ice to break it and get to its prey.

When food is really scarce, it will even eat its own poop!

STRANGEOMETER

 STRANGENESS 12/25

 DANGER 12/25

 CUNNING 15/25

 FEROCITY 13/25

 STRANGEOMETER SCORE 52/100

SOMETIMES MY WINTER COAT IS BLUE-GRAY IN COLOR.

ARCTIC FOX

This snowy white fox may look cute, but it's a vicious hunter, tracking down seal pups in their snow dens and eating them. Its white coat keeps it hidden in the snow so it can creep up on other animals like lemmings, voles, hares, and birds. It has also cleverly adapted to be able to keep warm at temperatures as low as −58°F (−50°C).

Its powerful venom is used to instantly stun or kill prey, like fish and shrimp, so that their struggle to escape doesn't damage the jellyfish's delicate tentacles.

More people have died from box jellyfish stings than shark bites in the past 50 years.

STRANGEOMETER

STRANGENESS		15/25
DANGER		25/25
CUNNING		8/25
FEROCITY		6/25
STRANGEOMETER SCORE		54/100

I'M FAST AND DEADLY!

BOX JELLYFISH

The box jellyfish's venom is among the most toxic in the world. It attacks the heart, nervous system, and skin of its prey.

Australia and Indo-Pacific

GREAT WHITE PELICAN

The great white pelican is one of the largest flying birds in the world and can be found fishing in shallow swamps in Africa. Its bill can grow up to 20 in. (50 cm) long and has a huge stretchy pouch underneath.

Africa, Southern Europe, and Asia

Pelicans need to eat more than 2.2 lb. (1 kg) of fish a day, and the birds sometimes work together to round up fish.

THEY SAY THAT I'VE GOT A BIG MOUTH. TRUE!

The pelican dips its long beak in the water, scooping up huge quantities of water and fish. It then closes its beak, tips its head back, squeezes the water out, and swallows the fish whole. When fish are scarce, pelicans may also eat other birds.

STRANGEOMETER

STRANGENESS		16/25
DANGER		12/25
CUNNING		12/25
FEROCITY		15/25
STRANGEOMETER SCORE		55/100

QUIZ

See if you can answer these questions on the ten predators you've just learned about!

3. How does a platypus inject venom?

How long does it take for a Venus flytrap to digest an insect?

4.

1. How does a box jellyfish stop its prey struggling?

2. What bird is this?

6. What is the name of the chemical reaction in glowworms that produces light?

7.

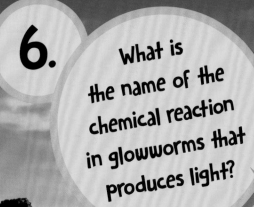

What predator is this?

5. How does a piranha scare other fish?

8. What do Arctic foxes eat when food is scarce?

9.

How much fish does a pelican eat every day?

10. How did the cobra lily get its name?

#30 BARN OWL

Barn owls hunt at night and have lots of features to ensure their success as predators. Their soft feathers muffle the sound of their flight so they can swoop down on prey in silence. They have excellent eyesight and one ear higher than the other to help them pinpoint where tiny sounds come from.

Barn owls eat mice, voles, shrews, and rats. They swallow them whole, then cough up a pellet containing the parts they can't digest, like fur and bones.

STRANGEOMETER

STRANGENESS	15/25
DANGER	10/25
CUNNING	18/25
FEROCITY	13/25
STRANGEOMETER SCORE	56/100

MY HEART-SHAPED FACE DIRECTS SOUND TO MY SENSITIVE EARS.

A pair of barn owls needs to catch about 5,000 items of prey a year to feed themselves and their family.

Every continent except Antarctica

Barn owls fly silently back and forth across a piece of ground until they hear the slightest noise, and then they pounce with deadly accuracy.

THE CLUE IS IN MY NAME. I'M A MONSTROUS PREDATOR!

STRANGEOMETER

 STRANGENESS 15/25

 DANGER 15/25

CUNNING 12/25

 FEROCITY 15/25

 STRANGEOMETER SCORE 57/100

A bite from a Gila is very painful, but don't try to shake the creature off. The best way to get it to let go is to dunk its head underwater.

GILA MONSTER

The Gila monster is one of the few venomous lizards. It grabs and holds onto its prey for up to 15 minutes while its venom attacks the nerves of its victim.

North America

The Gila swallows its prey alive if it's small or crushes it to death if it's bigger. It doesn't chew its food but swallows it whole. It can eat about a third of its body weight in one sitting and stores fat in its tail, which allows it to go up to a year without food.

PAUSSINAE BEETLE

Also known as the ant nest beetle, this crafty creature spends most of its life inside ants' nests, where it has a supply of its favorite food – ants and their larvae.

Instead of trying to get rid of the beetle, the ants use their large antennae to move it further into the nest. This is because the beetle secretes a substance that the ants love to eat and which calms them down.

STRANGEOMETER

STRANGENESS		19/25
DANGER		10/25
CUNNING		19/25
FEROCITY		10/25
STRANGEOMETER SCORE		58/100

Continental Africa, Madagascar, Southeast Asia, and Australia

Some beetles only ever leave the ants' nest to breed.

I IMITATE THE SOUND OF AN ANT QUEEN TO GET INTO THE NEST.

The bat has a heat sensor in its nose that tells it the best place to sink its teeth. It needs to drink about half its body weight in each 20–30-minute feeding.

Central and South America

STRANGEOMETER

👁 STRANGENESS		20/25
⚠ DANGER		10/25
👓 CUNNING		24/25
🦷 FEROCITY		5/25
⭐ STRANGEOMETER SCORE		59/100

VAMPIRE BAT

I SOMETIMES MIMIC A CHICK TO SNEAK UP ON HENS.

This tiny animal is the only mammal that feeds entirely on blood, and it does so without killing any of its prey. It drinks only enough blood for a meal, leaving plenty for next time.

Although it can fly, the bat approaches its prey (such as sleeping cattle or horses) along the ground, taking a small bite and lapping the blood like a cat. Its saliva prevents the blood from clotting while it feeds.

BARRACUDA

The fearsome-looking barracuda can swim at an astounding 25 mph (40 kph) to snatch fish such as groupers, anchovies, and snappers. It is attracted by shiny objects so tends to hunt prey with gold or silver scales.

The biggest barracuda can be more than 5 ft. (1.5 m) long. It will sometimes hide from its prey and ambush it, but if there is no cover, it will just chase it.

I'M MOST ACTIVE AT NIGHT, SO WATCH OUT WHEN IT GETS DARK.

Tropical and subtropical oceans

Its very sharp dagger-like teeth stop its prey from slipping out of its mouth once captured. It has been known to attack and bite swimmers.

STRANGEOMETER

👁 STRANGENESS		15/25
⚠ DANGER		18/25
👓 CUNNING		12/25
🦷 FEROCITY		15/25
⭐ STRANGEOMETER SCORE		60/100

BLUE-RINGED OCTOPUS

This small octopus can be found in tidal pools. It is only 5–8 in. (12–20 cm) in size but is one of the world's most venomous creatures. If annoyed, it will bite, and its venom can kill a human in minutes. There is no cure.

The octopus doesn't actually make its own venom. Scientists think that it's made by tiny microbes that grow in the octopus's salivary glands.

WHEN MY RINGS TURN BLUE, BACK OFF!

Pacific and Indian Oceans

This deadly octopus uses its venom to kill prey. It will pounce on crabs, shrimp, and fish, biting them with its parrot-like beak.

The blue rings of its name are a warning to stay away and are only seen if the animal is alarmed.

STRANGEOMETER

👁 STRANGENESS		14/25
⚠ DANGER		25/25
👓 CUNNING		7/25
🔥 FEROCITY		15/25
⭐ STRANGEOMETER SCORE		61/100

Its clever trick is to mimic the sound of a young tamarin monkey. The call attracts adult tamarin monkeys, who come closer to investigate, and the margay can then attack. Although the mimicry isn't very good, it works well enough to get the monkeys' attention.

I'M THE IMPRESSIONIST OF THE CAT WORLD.

STRANGEOMETER

STRANGENESS		15/25
DANGER		12/25
CUNNING		22/25
FEROCITY		13/25
STRANGEOMETER SCORE		62/100

The margay can turn its back legs 180 degrees to allow it to run head-first down a tree, like a squirrel. It can also hang from a branch with one foot.

Mexico, Central and South America

MARGAY

One of the smaller big cats, the cunning margay lives in forests where it feeds on mammals, birds, and fruit.

TRAPDOOR SPIDER

Not all spiders spin webs. The trapdoor spider hides in a hole camouflaged with sticks and leaves, and grabs insects that pass by. Some even make their burrows next to streams to catch fish.

Americas, Africa, China, Japan, and Australia

KNOCK, KNOCK. WHO'S THERE? ONLY CREEPY LITTLE ME!

The spider hides behind its trapdoor and waits to feel vibrations from passing prey. It then leaps out and drags its dinner back into the hole.

STRANGEOMETER

👁 STRANGENESS		22/25
⚠ DANGER		10/25
👓 CUNNING		21/25
🦷 FEROCITY		10/25
☆ STRANGEOMETER SCORE		63/100

Female trapdoor spiders remain in or near their burrows for most of their lives and have to make the hole bigger as they grow.

Its saw is packed with sensory organs that detect tiny electrical signals made by fish swimming nearby. It uses its saw to attack and stun the fish before gobbling them up.

MY SAW HELPS ME TO FIND FISH AND THEN STUN THEM.

SAWFISH

The sawfish has a ferocious-looking nose called a rostrum that really does look like a double-sided saw. Adult sawfish can grow up to 23 ft. (7 m) long, and the saw part can be a quarter of its length.

The rostrum can also be used like a shovel to dig for prey in the muddy seafloor. Unfortunately, sawfish are now one of the most endangered species in the world.

Tropical Atlantic and Pacific

STRANGEOMETER

STRANGENESS		21/25
DANGER		15/25
CUNNING		15/25
FEROCITY		13/25
STRANGEOMETER SCORE		64/100

Baby sawfish are born with their saws covered in a protective material so that they don't injure their mother.

#21

Although this fiesty frog doesn't have sharp claws, it has a massive mouth to cram its prey into after ambushing it.

Africa

When the weather gets too hot and dry, the frog stays in a hole underground. It can be there for up to a year, so it's not surprising that it is so hungry when it comes out.

STRANGEOMETER

STRANGENESS		10/25
DANGER		17/25
CUNNING		17/25
FEROCITY		21/25
STRANGEOMETER SCORE		65/100

I'LL EAT ALMOST ANYTHING THAT I CAN FIT INTO MY MOUTH.

AFRICAN BULLFROG

This aggressive amphibian will eat spiders, scorpions, rodents, snakes, fish, and pretty much anything else it can swallow, including other frogs.

QUIZ

See if you can answer these questions on the ten predators you've just learned about!

1. What is this bird?

2. How do you get a Gila monster to release its grip?

3. What animal feeds entirely on blood?

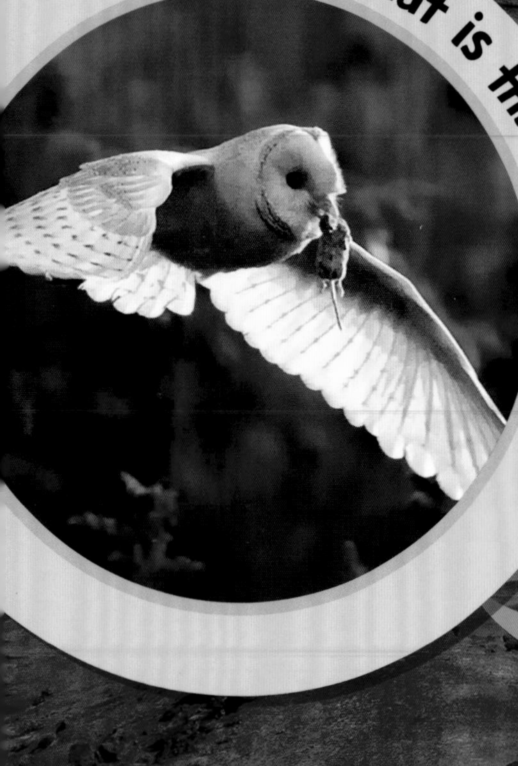

4. How do ants move the paussinae beetle?

6.

What predator is this?

What animal does the margay mimic?

8.

7.

5.

How fast can a barracuda swim?

How long can a giant African bullfrog stay underground?

10.

How does the trapdoor spider know its prey is approaching?

9.

What do you call a sawfish's nose?

ANSWERS

1. BARN OWL 2. DUNK IT IN WATER 3. VAMPIRE BAT 4. WITH ITS ANTENNAE
5. 25 MPH (40 KPH) 6. BLUE-RINGED OCTOPUS 7. THE TAMARIN MONKEY
8. UP TO A YEAR 9. IT FEELS VIBRATIONS 10. A ROSTRUM

Although the Komodo dragon has long claws and a muscular tail that it can whip, it attacks its prey by biting it with sharp teeth, and injecting venom that gradually kills the animal.

Indonesia

I USE MY LONG TONGUE TO SMELL THE AIR AND FIND MY DINNER.

The dragon can smell a dead or dying animal almost 6 mi. (10 km) away. It holds its prey using its razor-sharp claws and tears off chunks of meat that it swallows whole. It can also unhinge its jaws to eat animals the size of a goat in one gulp.

STRANGEOMETER

👁 STRANGENESS		18/25
⚠ DANGER		19/25
👓 CUNNING		14/25
🐾 FEROCITY		15/25
⭐ STRANGEOMETER SCORE		66/100

KOMODO DRAGON

The world's heaviest lizard lives in Indonesia and mainly eats rotting meat from dead animals. Although it can grow to more than 8 ft. (2.5 m) long, it can run at 12.5 mph (20 kph) to catch birds, monkeys, pigs, goats, and larger creatures such as buffalo and deer.

South America

STRANGEOMETER

 STRANGENESS — 23/25

 DANGER — 13/25

 CUNNING — 13/25

 FEROCITY — 18/25

 STRANGEOMETER SCORE — 67/100

This super-strange centipede has more than 20 pairs of legs. It will climb the walls of caves and hang by these legs to catch bats.

AMAZONIAN GIANT
CENTIPEDE

This giant creepy-crawly grows to more than 12 in. (30 cm) long and uses venomous claws to capture rodents, insects, and lizards. The poison is lethal to most small prey and will even make a human feel ill.

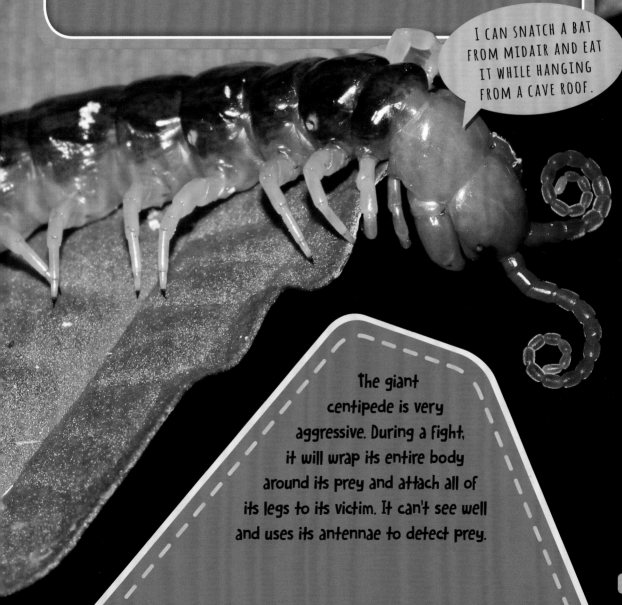

I CAN SNATCH A BAT FROM MIDAIR AND EAT IT WHILE HANGING FROM A CAVE ROOF.

The giant centipede is very aggressive. During a fight, it will wrap its entire body around its prey and attach all of its legs to its victim. It can't see well and uses its antennae to detect prey.

#18

the tasmanian devil can make a scary screeching noise, but when it is scared, it seems to yawn and produces a terrible smell.

I'M A PINT-SIZED MENACE. DON'T MESS WITH ME!

STRANGEOMETER

STRANGENESS		18/25
DANGER		17/25
CUNNING		14/25
FEROCITY		19/25
STRANGEOMETER SCORE		68/100

Tasmania

It is one of the largest carnivorous marsupials in the world and a relative of the kangaroo.

TASMANIAN DEVIL

Although it looks cute, the tasmanian devil has bone-crunching jaws, giving it one of the strongest bites of any mammal on Earth. It eats anything from insects to wallabies, and will even eat fur and bones.

TENTACLED SNAKE

This strange-looking snake specializes in catching fish and is a master of ambush.

Southeast Asia

I CAN STAY UNDERWATER FOR UP TO 30 MINUTES TO CATCH FISH.

It lies still in the water pretending to be a tree branch. When a fish swims near, it moves its tail to scare the fish into moving in the direction of its mouth. It then eats it so quickly that scientists can only see the attack by filming it with a special slow-motion camera.

STRANGEOMETER

STRANGENESS		22/25
DANGER		11/25
CUNNING		25/25
FEROCITY		11/25
STRANGEOMETER SCORE		69/100

#16

Arctic

Its thick white coat camouflages it and also helps keep it warm. The bears wait on the sea ice for seals to come to the surface to breathe, before grabbing them.

I LOOK CUDDLY, BUT I'M DEADLY. IF YOU COME TOO CLOSE TO MY CUBS, I CAN KNOCK YOUR HEAD OFF WITH ONE SWIPE OF MY PAW.

STRANGEOMETER

 STRANGENESS   11/25

 DANGER   23/25

 CUNNING   15/25

 FEROCITY   21/25

 STRANGEOMETER SCORE   70/100

POLAR BEAR

The polar bear is the largest land-based carnivore, with adult males weighing up to 1,500 lb. (700 kg). Its favorite food is seals, and it can smell them beneath 3.3 ft. (1 m) of ice and from almost 0.6 mi. (1 km) away.

Polar bears are excellent swimmers and can stay in the icy waters of the Arctic for hours in search of food.

STONEFISH

The stonefish won't win many awards
for beauty, but it is perfectly adapted
to capture its favorite prey of
shrimp and small fish.
Its camouflage helps it blend
in with the rocks or coral
reefs, where it lies waiting
to gobble up prey in
an astonishingly quick
time of 0.015
seconds.

Stonefish are
the most venomous fish
known. They lie buried in the
sand and can shoot poison through
13 spines on their backs. Amazingly,
stonefish can survive out of water
for more than 24 hours.

I'M HIDING FROM THE
LARGE SHARKS THAT ARE
IMMUNE TO MY VENOM
AND WILL EAT ME.

The stonefish is actually eaten as a delicacy by people in China and Japan, as the venom becomes harmless when cooked.

Pacific and Indian Oceans

STRANGEOMETER

STRANGENESS		20/25
DANGER		20/25
CUNNING		20/25
FEROCITY		11/25
STRANGEOMETER SCORE		71/100

There are about 300 triangular teeth in a great white's massive mouth. It shakes its head from side to side to help its teeth saw through its prey.

STRANGEOMETER

👁 STRANGENESS		11/25
⚠ DANGER		22/25
👓 CUNNING		18/25
🦷 FEROCITY		21/25
⭐ STRANGEOMETER SCORE		72/100

The great white can reach speeds of 25 mph (40 kph) and uses this speed to attack seals. It swims quickly toward them from the deep, grabbing them out of the water in an action known as breaching, when the shark jumps right out of the sea.

Coastal and temperate waters

I'M RESPONSIBLE FOR MORE SHARK ATTACKS THAN ANY OTHER SPECIES.

GREAT WHITE SHARK

This monster of the sea is around 16 ft. (5 m) long and can smell blood 3 mi. (5 km) away. Its diet consists of tuna, rays, seals, whales, and even other sharks.

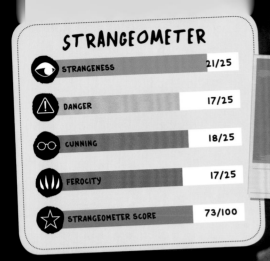

STRANGEOMETER

STRANGENESS		21/25
DANGER		17/25
CUNNING		18/25
FEROCITY		17/25
STRANGEOMETER SCORE		73/100

North America

MY JAWS SNAP SO QUICKLY THAT I CAN BITE OFF YOUR FINGERS. WATCH OUT!

It is one of the largest freshwater turtles and can grow to weigh more than 220 lb. (100 kg). the turtle is not fussy about food and will eat frogs, snakes, snails, crayfish, and even other turtles.

ALLIGATOR SNAPPING TURTLE

this scary looking turtle has a bright red tip on the end of its tongue that looks like a worm. It uses it to attract fish or frogs. It lies still in the water with its mouth open and quickly snaps its jaws shut when its prey close.

#12

Flying above the forest, the eagle listens for the sounds of monkeys and then skillfully swoops through the trees to attack. Its strong talons wound the prey and help the eagle carry it away. There are even reports of these eagles carrying off children.

STRANGEOMETER

 STRANGENESS | 15/25

 DANGER | 21/25

 CUNNING | 15/25

 FEROCITY | 23/25

 STRANGEOMETER SCORE | 74/100

Africa

54

AFRICAN CROWNED EAGLE

The crowned eagle is one of the most powerful birds of prey in the world. It mainly attacks and eats mammals, particularly monkeys.

MY WINGSPAN CAN BE UP TO 6 FT. (1.8 M), AND I CAN WEIGH NEARLY 11 LB. (5 KG).

Crowned eagles mate for life and keep the same nest, too. They add new sticks and leaves to it every year until it is up to 10 ft. (3 m) high.

Atlantic, Pacific, Indian Oceans and Red Sea

FROGFISH

The frogfish can resemble rocks, coral, or sponges, so its prey doesn't see it until it's too late. In just six milliseconds, it can open its huge mouth and suck fish in, closing its throat so that the catch can't escape. Its stomach can expand, too, allowing the frogfish to eat fish twice its size.

The frogfish blends into coral or rocks, dangling a special fin in front of it, which attracts the fish that it eats.

STRANGEOMETER

 STRANGENESS — 22/25

 DANGER — 14/25

 CUNNING — 24/25

 FEROCITY — 15/25

⭐ **STRANGEOMETER SCORE** — 75/100

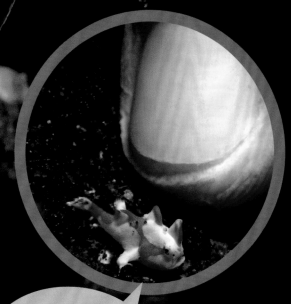

I'M A TINY FROGFISH, BUT SOME OF US CAN BE 16 IN. (40 CM) LONG.

QUIZ

What predator is this?

4.

1. How quickly can a frogfish gobble up its prey?

2. What does the Komodo dragon do with its tongue?

3. How long can tentacled snakes stay underwater?

6. What creatures are immune to stonefish venom and can eat them?

What is it called when sharks jump right out of the sea?

7.

8.

5. What is a polar bear's favorite food?

What bird is this?

10.

9. How does the alligator snapping turtle attract prey?

What does the tasmanian devil do when scared?

STRANGEOMETER

 STRANGENESS 23/25

 DANGER 20/25

 CUNNING 20/25

 FEROCITY 13/25

 STRANGEOMETER SCORE 76/100

South America

Like many snakes, the anaconda can unhook its jaws to allow it to swallow its prey whole, even if it is a large animal, such as a pig, deer, or caiman (a member of the alligator family). After such a big meal, it may not need to eat again for months.

The anaconda is a great swimmer and can hold its breath underwater for ten minutes.

I'M WAITING FOR MY LATEST CRUSH!

ANACONDA

The green anaconda is the largest snake in the world. It is non-venomous and captures its prey by lying in wait in water, then pouncing and wrapping its coils around the prey and squeezing.

CHIMPANZEE

Although chimpanzees mainly eat fruit and vegetables, they also have a taste for meat and will hunt their favorite prey, such as the red colobus monkey. In one area of Uganda, the chimpanzees hunted so many of the monkeys that they almost disappeared.

STRANGEOMETER

 STRANGENESS 10/25

 DANGER 23/25

 CUNNING 19/25

 FEROCITY 25/25

STRANGEOMETER SCORE 77/100

Chimpanzees are very clever and make tools to help them eat, such as sticks to pick up insects and stones to break open nuts.

I'M ABOUT ONE-AND-A-HALF TIMES STRONGER THAN A HUMAN. DO YOU WANT TO ARM WRESTLE?

Africa

Chimps may appear mischievous and funny, but they are incredibly strong and can be very aggressive. Collectively, they can plan attacks on other groups of chimps and may even eat their enemies.

#8

Crocodiles really do cry "crocodile tears"! When they eat, they sometimes swallow too much air, which makes their eyes water.

Americas, tropical regions of Africa, Asia, and Australia

STRANGEOMETER

STRANGENESS	15/25
 **DANGER**	23/25
CUNNING	18/25
FEROCITY	22/25
⭐ **STRANGEOMETER SCORE**	78/100

the muscles that close a crocodile's mouth are much stronger than those that open it, so you can hold a croc's mouth shut with your hands. Do you want to try?

WOULD YOU LIKE TO JOIN ME FOR A BITE?

CROCODILE

The crocodile is a relative of both dinosaurs and birds. With its sharp teeth, it has the most powerful bite in the animal world, 25 times stronger than a human's bite. It hunts by patiently waiting for its prey to come near and then pouncing. After grabbing the animal, it goes into a "death roll," spinning around to rip off parts of its victim and swallowing them whole.

The electric eel can generate 500 volts of electricity, enough to light up a Christmas tree. The electricity is produced by special organs in the fish's body.

The eel can leap out of the water to attack an animal it thinks is a threat. This allows it to deliver an even bigger shock, as its electricity is more powerful out of the water.

CAN I GIVE YOU A BUZZ?

South America

STRANGEOMETER

STRANGENESS	25/25
DANGER	23/25
CUNNING	15/25
FEROCITY	16/25
STRANGEOMETER SCORE	79/100

ELECTRIC EEL

Despite the name, electric eels are not eels, but fish. They live in the murky waters of the Amazon and can't see very well. Instead, they detect prey with weak electrical signals that act like radar, and then use a bigger zap of electricity to stun the prey.

SPIDER-TAILED HORNED VIPER

Several snakes use their tails to attract prey, but the spider-tailed horned viper has the strangest one of all. The tip of its tail looks just like a spider, and the snake flicks it about to attract birds.

STRANGEOMETER

👁 STRANGENESS		23/25
⚠ DANGER		18/25
👓 CUNNING		22/25
🦷 FEROCITY		17/25
⭐ STRANGEOMETER SCORE		80/100

THE GOOD NEWS IS THAT I'M NOT VENOMOUS.

The viper is so well camouflaged that a bird flies straight for its tail and doesn't see its jaws until it is too late. The viper strikes at lightning speed and bites down on the bird's neck to kill it. The only problem is that the tail is so lifelike that in some cases, it gets pecked right off.

Iran

67

A clever hunter, the great grey shrike can mimic the calls of other birds to attract them before pouncing.

I USUALLY EAT THE FOOD THAT I STORE WITHIN NINE DAYS.

GREAT GREY SHRIKE

This little bird doesn't look like much of a predator, but it is not called the "butcher bird" for nothing. Not only is it a meat-eater, but it also saves its kills to eat later by impaling them on thorns.

The bird sometimes catches lizards and frogs but usually leaves them impaled on spikes and doesn't eat them.

Europe and Asia

STRANGEOMETER

STRANGENESS		23/25
DANGER		17/25
CUNNING		18/25
FEROCITY		23/25
STRANGEOMETER SCORE		81/100

The shrike is a relative of the crow and sits on top of trees or telephone poles looking for insects, mice, other birds, frogs, and even stoats. It swoops down on its prey and hits it on the skull with its hooked beak.

PIRATE SPIDER

Pirate spiders have lost the ability to spin webs, so they have a very clever way of catching their food... using other spiders.

The smart pirate spider tricks other spiders by twanging their webs and then pouncing on them when they come to investigate.

Pirate spiders' venom works best on other spiders and is less effective on insects.

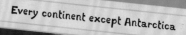

Every continent except Antarctica

I CAN ONLY ATTACK ANOTHER SPIDER IF IT MAKES A WEB.

The pirate spider then traps the other spider with its two long front legs and bites it, injecting a venom to kill it.

STRANGEOMETER

 STRANGENESS 24/25

 DANGER 17/25

 CUNNING 23/25

 FEROCITY 18/25

 STRANGEOMETER SCORE 82/100

#3

Morays work with other fish, like groupers, to hunt. The eel chases the prey from the rocks, then the groupers stop the prey from swimming away.

I CAN TIE MY BODY IN KNOTS TO SQUASH MY FOOD AND MAKE IT EASIER TO SWALLOW.

The deadly moray eel has two sets of jaws. One is for holding its prey, while the other shoots forward from its throat to help it swallow its prey. Its jaws are very powerful, and some divers have lost fingers trying to feed a moray by hand – it doesn't have very good eyesight and can bite fingers off by mistake.

MORAY EEL

Morays are quite shy and hide in crevices or under rocks waiting for prey to ambush, such as fish, crabs, squid, cuttlefish, and mollusks.

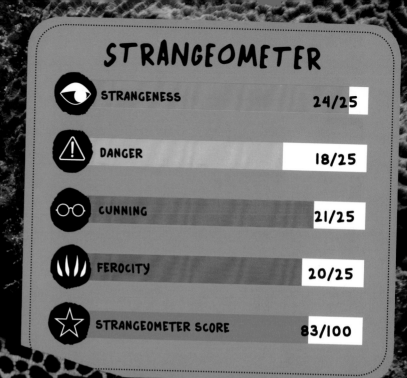

STRANGEOMETER

👁 STRANGENESS		24/25
⚠ DANGER		18/25
👓 CUNNING		21/25
🦷 FEROCITY		20/25
⭐ STRANGEOMETER SCORE		83/100

Temperate and tropical waters
in every ocean

TARANTULA HAWK

At about 2 in. (5 cm) long, the tarantula hawk is one of the biggest wasps and looks terrifying. As its name suggests, its prey is the tarantula spider, but it doesn't eat it...

The tarantula hawk attacks and stings a tarantula, stunning it. The wasp then drags it to a hole, where it lays an egg in the tarantula's abdomen before burying it alive. The wasp larva feeds on the living tarantula until it is ready to go into the world.

The sting of the tarantula hawk wasp is one of the most painful in the insect world. One expert said the best thing to do if you get stung is to lie on the floor and scream for three minutes until the pain passes!

I SNEAK UP ON A TARANTULA AND FLIP IT OVER SO I CAN FIND A WEAK SPOT TO STING.

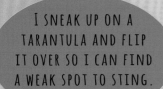

Americas, Africa, Asia, Australia

STRANGEOMETER

	STRANGENESS	25/25
DANGER		20/25
CUNNING		23/25
FEROCITY		20/25
STRANGEOMETER SCORE		88/100

1

HONEY
BADGER

This ferocious relative of the weasel and the skunk will eat most things, and is brave enough to attack poisonous snakes, such as cobras. It has even been known to chase lions away from their food.

The honey badger has very powerful jaws, which enable it to crunch bones and even tortoise shells. Its skin and hair are very thick, which protects it from animals silly enough to try and attack it.

STRANGEOMETER

STRANGENESS		23/25
DANGER		20/25
CUNNING		21/25
FEROCITY		25/25
STRANGEOMETER SCORE		89/100

I'M FEROCIOUS, STRONG, AND MAKE A BIG STINK. NICE TO MEET YOU!

Africa and Asia

As its name suggests, it loves honey! It uses a gland at the base of its tail to drop a "stink bomb" that makes bees unable to defend their hive while the honey badger eats its fill.

QUIZ

See if you can answer these questions on the ten predators you've just learned about!

3. Why do crocodiles cry?

How many volts of electricity can an electric eel produce?

1. How long can an anaconda hold its breath underwater?

4.

What predator is this?

2.

6. Where could you find the spider-tailed horned viper?

7. What can't pirate spiders do that most spiders can?

8. How does the honey badger make bees unable to defend their hives?

5. What is the great grey shrike sometimes called?

What predator is this?

9.

10. What does the moray eel have two of?

ANSWERS

1. 10 MINUTES 2. CHIMPANZEE 3. BECAUSE THEY HAVE SWALLOWED TOO MUCH AIR WHEN EATING 4. 500 VOLTS 5. THE BUTCHER BIRD 6. IRAN 7. SPIN A WEB 8. IT DROPS A STINK BOMB 9. TARANTULA HAWK 10. SETS OF JAWS

GLOSSARY

camouflage	a way of making something look like its surroundings so it can't be seen
amphibian	a cold-blooded creature that can live on land or in water
antennae	the feelers on the heads of insects or crustaceans
carnivore	an animal that eats meat
carnivorous	meat-eating
coral	a marine animal that stays in one place under the sea and forms a hard, rock-like substance
digest	to break down food inside the stomach
fang	a large pointed tooth
gland	an organ in the body that produces substances that help the body function
larva	a grub or caterpillar, hatched from an egg; the young form of many insects
mammal	warm-blooded animals that breathe air; the females have glands that produce milk for their young
marsupial	a mammal that carries its young in a pouch, such as a kangaroo
microbe	a tiny organism (living thing); often harmful or disease-bearing
organ	a part of the body
prey	an animal that is hunted and eaten by other animals
radar	an electronic system used to detect the position of things
rodent	a small mammal with long, sharp front teeth
saliva	the clear liquid found inside the mouth
shoal	a large group of fish swimming together
talon	the claw of an animal or bird
venom	a poison released by some snakes and insects